RECOVERING A BODY

Helen Dunmore was born in 1952 in Beverley, Yorkshire. After studying English at York University, she taught in Finland for two years. She lives in Bristol, and works as a freelance writer of poetry, poems for children, short stories and novels, and has been Writer-in-Residence at the University of Glamorgan since 1990.

Helen Dunmore has published five books of poems, all with Bloodaxe: *The Apple Fall* (1983), *The Sea Skater* (1986), *The Raw Garden* (1988), *Short Days, Long Nights: New & Selected Poems* (1991) and *Recovering a Body* (1994). She won the Alice Hunt Bartlett Award for *The Sea Skater* in 1987. *The Raw Garden* was made a Poetry Book Society Choice, and *Short Days, Long Nights* a Poetry Book Society Recommendation. In 1989 she won second prize in the *Times Literary Supplement*/Cheltenham Literature Festival Poetry Competition, and in 1990 first prize in the Cardiff International Poetry Competition.

She has published two novels with Viking Penguin, *Zennor in Darkness* (1993) and *Burning Bright* (1994); two novels for young people with Julia MacRae, *Going to Egypt* (1992) and *In the Money* (1993); and a book of children's poems, *Secrets* (Bodley Head, 1994).

RECOVERING
A BODY

HELEN DUNMORE

BLOODAXE BOOKS

ISBN: 1 85224 289 2

First published 1994 by
Bloodaxe Books Ltd,
P.O. Box 1SN,
Newcastle upon Tyne NE99 1SN.

Bloodaxe Books Ltd acknowledges
the financial assistance of Northern Arts.

Cover printing by J. Thomson Colour Printers Ltd, Glasgow.

Printed in Great Britain by
Cromwell Press Ltd, Broughton Gifford, Melksham, Wiltshire.

Acknowledgements

Acknowledgements are due to the editors of the following publications in which some of these poems first appeared: *The Forward Book of Poetry 1993* (Forward Publishing, 1992), *The Independent, The Independent on Sunday, London Magazine, New Statesman & Society, Planet, Poetry Review, Poetry with an Edge* (Bloodaxe Books, new edition, 1993), *The Printer's Devil, Second Shift, Sixty Women Poets* (Bloodaxe Books, 1993), *Stand, The Spectator, Verse, Writers on the Storm* and *Writing Women*.

Contents

To Virgil

Lead me with your cold, sure hand,
make me press the correct buttons
on the automatic ticket machine,
make me not present my ticket upside down
to the slit mouth at the barriers,

then make the lift not jam
in the hot dark of the deepest lines.
May I hear the voice on the loudspeaker
and understand each syllable
of the doggerel of stations.

If it is rush-hour, let me be close to the doors,
I do not ask for space,
let no one crush me into a corner
or accidentally squeeze hard on my breasts
or hit me with bags or chew gum in my face.

If there are incidents, let them be over,
let there be no red-and-white tape
marking the place, make it not happen
when the tunnel has wrapped its arms around my train
and the lights have failed.

Float me up the narrow escalator
not looking backward, losing my balance
or letting go of your cold, sure hand.
Let there not be a fire
in the gaps, hold me secure.
Let me come home to the air.

Three Ways of Recovering a Body

By chance I was alone in my bed the morning
I woke to find my body had gone.
It had been coming. I'd cut off my hair in sections
so each of you would have something to remember,
then my nails worked loose from their beds
of oystery flesh. Who was it got them?
One night I slipped out of my skin. It lolloped
hooked to my heels, hurting. I had to spray on
more scent so you could find me in the dark,
I was going so fast. One of you begged for my ears
because you could hear the sea in them.

First I planned to steal myself back. I was a mist
on thighs, belly and hips. I'd slept with so many men.
I was with you in the ash-haunted stations of Poland,
I was with you on that grey plaza in Berlin
while you wolfed three doughnuts without stopping,
thinking yourself alone. Soon I recovered my lips
by waiting behind the mirror while you shaved.
You pouted. I peeled away kisses like wax
no longer warm to the touch. Then I flew off.

Next I decided to become a virgin. Without a body
it was easy to make up a new story. In seven years
every invisible cell would be renewed
and none of them would have touched any of you.
I went to a cold lake, to a grey-lichened island,
I was gold in the wallet of the water.
I was known to the inhabitants, who were in love
with the coveted whisper of my virginity:
all too soon they were bringing me coffee and perfume,
cash under stones. I could really do something for them.

Thirdly I tried marriage to a good husband
who knew my past but forgave it. I believed in the power
of his penis to smoke out all those men
so that bit by bit my body service would resume,
although for a while I'd be the one woman in the world
who was only present in the smile of her vagina.
He stroked the air where I might have been.
I turned to the mirror and saw mist gather
as if someone lived in the glass. Recovering
I breathed to myself, *'Hold on! I'm coming.'*

Holiday to Lonely

He's going on holiday to lonely
but no one knows. He has got the sunblock
the cash and the baseball cap
shorts that looked nice in the shop
then two days' indoor bicycling
to get his legs ready.

He plans to learn something in lonely.
Bits of the language, new dishes.
He would like to try out a sport –
jet-ski maybe, or fishing.
You are meant to be alone, fishing.
There are books about it at the airport.

In the departure lounge, he has three hours
to learn to harpoon a marlin
and to overhear the history
of that couple quarrelling
about Bourbon and Jamesons –
which is the best way to have fun.

He is starting to like the look of lonely
with its steady climate, its goals
anyone can touch. He settles
for drinking lots of Aqua Libra
and being glad about Airmiles
as the Australian across the aisle
plugs into *Who's That Girl?*

Poem in a Hotel

Waiting. I'm here waiting
like a cable-car caught in a thunderstorm.
At six someone will feed me, at seven
I'll stroll and sit by the band.

I have never seen so many trombones
taking the air, or so many mountains.
Under them there are tunnels
to a troll's salt-garden.

The lake is a dirty thumb-mark.
If nowhere has a middle
this lake is its navel,
pregnant with sickeningly large carp.

Bent as if travelling backwards, the birches
wipe the cheeks of 29 parasols.
A little girl scythes at her shuttlecock:
4, 6, 7 strokes –

there are 29 bright parasols
outfacing the sun
and the little girl wears a red cap
to blunt her vision.

I lie through half a morning
with my eyelids gummed down,
neither rising nor falling
until the next meal comes round.

I keep a straw in my mouth
so I can breathe,
I am drinking Sprite in a hotel,
I am a carp in the reeds.

The Bike Lane

Of course they're dead, or this is a film.
Along the promenade the sun
moves down council-painted white lanes –

these are for cycling. On the other hand
the sea is going quietly out to France,
taking its time. If the cliffs are white,

iron stanchions are planted in them
so a bleed of rust can be seen
by the army rafting its way in

on lilos and pedalos. Professional cyclists
walk with one hand on the saddle,
waiting to be told to put on

red vests which show up in the race.
The aisle of the falling tide
squints to infinity, the bike-lane

is much in need of repainting
like the smile of the sea-front towards France.
In the less-than-shelter of the beach huts

two people I love are waiting
with as much infinity in their laps
as you can catch with a red vest on.

The cyclists flash past them –
one turns his keyed-up white face
but they are dead and this is a film.

Drink and the Devil

On his skin the stink
of last night turned
to acetaldehyde.
What comes through the curtains must be light.
It combs the shadows of his brain
and frightens him.

Things not to think of crowd in.
The things she said
as if sick of saying them.
The jumpy blanks in what happened.
The way he skidded and there
was the kid looking,

staring through the bars of the landing
so I shouted *Monkey, Monkey*
and danced but he wouldn't laugh.
Or was that in the club?
I would never harm a hair
on the head of him.
If she doesn't know that she knows nothing.

The Senses

Years of seeing things. It was much too long
before I stopped believing in them:

poor eyesight, young parents.
The answer lay in the senses.

Look through those glasses. What do you see? Light?
Do you see light now? And now? More light?

The world sprang into focus
street lamps ballooned and balanced

sunlight glittered on the Bendix
each cloud was cut to perfection.

Years of hearing things. I must have been seven
before I stopped counting them

and then there was a teacher's note from school:
We don't think Helen is hearing anything at all.

They should have looked behind the sofa
where I'd be cuddling antlers

of Stag's Head Sumac, snapped from the tree,
its white sap dripping down my cardi.

I lay on my father's chest while he poured warm oil
and stopped my ears with cotton wool,

my antlers became antennae
my ear was laid to the ground of the prairie.

He turned me into a diviner,
seventy times seven was my answer.

Missing things was no problem.
I bisected the lines of sight and hearing

and made my nest in the classroom
just out of sight, just out of hearing,

where the teacher echoed with colour
like a soft-lipped moose in a meadow
stirring its bulk, which I knew
was lighter than a flower.

Hearing Things

That was the sound we heard in the wood
when it was growing dark
and adult voices calling us home
were thin and disbelieving.

In a murk of wild garlic
we nailed down slats for the roof of our house.
We would sleep out
long before the warmth of summer
in the wildness of spring,

we would mash the smoke of bluebells to slime
going in and out of our house.
Tall white-clothed trees were moving above us
like women in petticoats circling the table,
and chestnut candles stood still as thunder.

The nails never went home
as the hammer leapt in our hands,
from time to time we heard bells ringing
but thought nothing of them.

Ahvenanmaa

Breast to breast against the azaleas
they pitch, father and daughter,

the sun throws itself down
golden, glittering,

pale orange petals clutter their hair
as he catches her shoulders,

braced, they grapple and bruise
among the perfumed azaleas.

The flowers loll out their tongues,
tigers on dark stems

while breast to breast against the azaleas
they pitch, father and daughter.

The ferry slides between islands.
Pale and immediate, the sun rises.

The hull noses white marker-posts
glittering in summer water –

here, now, the channel deepens,
the sky darkens. Too cold in her dress

the girl scutters. Engine vents veil
steam while rain hides Ahvenanmaa.

Rubbing Down the Horse

The thing about a saddle is that second
you see it so closely, sweat-grains
pointing the leather,
pulled stitching and all, and the pommel gone black
and reins wrapped over themselves.
You see it so closely
because you have one foot in the stirrup
and someone else has your heel in his hand.
Your heel in someone else's hand

that second before they lift you, your face
turned to the saddle, the sweat marks
and smell of the horse, those stitches pulling
the way they tug and tear in your flesh
when you lie there in pain,
the hooves of it cutting,
trying to pin down the place, the time.
The nurse has your heel in her hand
yellow and still, already tender
though on Friday you were walking.

She is taking a pinprick
or else slowly, bit by bit, washing
your wrapped body from the heels upward
and talking, always talking.
She might want to ask someone
what way you would move when sunlight
filled the cobbles like straw,
or how without looking at it
you'd kick in place a zinc bucket
then bend and rub down the horse.

You came back to life in its sweetness

You came back to life in its sweetness,
to keen articulations of the knee joint,
to slow replays of balls kicking home
and the gape of the goalkeeper.

You came back to life in its sweetness,
to the smell of sweat, the night-blue
unwrinkling of the iris,
and going from table to table at parties.

Perhaps you'll waltz
on some far-off anniversary
with an elderly woman
who doesn't exist yet,

and you, you'll forget,
for now we're counting in years,
where we were counting in hours.

Heimat

Deep in busy lizzies and black iron
he sleeps for the Heimat,
and his photograph slips in and out of sight
as if breathing.

There are petals against his cheeks
but he is not handsome.
His small eyes search the graveyard fretfully
and the flesh of his cheeks clouds
the bones of heroism.

No one can stop him being young
and he is so tired of being young.
He would like to feel pain in his joints
as he wanders down to Hübers,
but he's here as always,
always on his way back from the photographer's
in his army collar
with a welt on his neck rubbed raw.

The mountains are white and sly as they always were.
Old women feed the graveyard with flowers,
clear the glass on his photograph
with chamois leathers,
bend and whisper the inscription.
They are his terrible suitors.

In the Desert Knowing Nothing

Here I am in the desert knowing nothing,
here I am knowing nothing
in the desert of knowing nothing,
here I am in this wide
desert long after midnight

here I am knowing nothing
hearing the noise of the rain
and the melt of fat in the pan

here is our man on the phone knowing something
and here's our man fresh from the briefing
in combat jeans and a clip microphone
testing for sound,
catching the desert rain, knowing something,

here's the general who's good with his men
storming the camera, knowing something
in the pit of his Americanness
here's the general taut in his battledress
and knowing something

here's the boy washing his kit in a tarpaulin
on a front-line he knows from his GCSE
coursework on Wilfrid Owen
and knowing something

here is the plane banking,
the *go go go* of adrenalin
the child melting
and here's the grass that grows overnight
from the desert rain, feeling for him
and knowing everything

and here I am knowing nothing
in the desert of knowing nothing
dry from not speaking.

Poem on the Obliteration of 100,000 Iraqi Soldiers

They are hiding away in the desert,
hiding in sand which is growing warm
with the hot season,

they are hiding from bone-wagons
and troops in protective clothing
who will not look at them,

the crowds were appalled on seeing him,
so disfigured did he look
that he seemed no longer human.

That killed head straining through the windscreen
with its frill of bubbles in the eye-sockets
is not trying to tell you something –

it is telling you something.
Do not look away,
permit them, permit them –

they are telling their names to the Marines
in one hundred thousand variations,
but no one is counting,

do not turn away,

for God is counting
all of us who are silent
holding our newspapers up, hiding.

Poem for a Satellite

The snow puts its hands over our eyes —
what does it hide
from us, what does it hide
from a winking satellite
slung in its string bag
across the path of sunlight and moonlight?

An orange in a net of stars —
spiked with electronics
sly as a grandma pretending
she can't find us
when it's easy-peasy.
I'm coming! Coo-eee!

Stop. Listen. They're looking
to the stars for intelligence.
Let it snow more
like a hand wiping away the lines
of sickness, the bird-black
lines of communication.

The Yellow Sky

That morning when the potato tops rusted,
the mangle rested and the well ran dry
and the turf house leaned like a pumpkin
against the yellow sky

there was a fire lit in the turf house
and a thin noise of crying,
and under the skinny sheets a woman
wadded with cloth against bleeding.

That morning her man went to the fields
after a shy pause at the end of her bed,
trying not to pick out the smell of her blood,
but she turned and was quiet.

All day the yellow sky walked on the turves
and she thought of things heavy to handle,
her dreams sweated with burdens,
the bump and grind of her mangle.

All day the child creaked in her cradle
like a fire as it sinks
and the woman crooned when she was able
across the impossible inches.

At that moment at the horizon there came a horseman
pressed to the saddle, galloping, galloping
fast as the whoop of an ambulance siren –
and just as unlikely. What happened

was slower and all of a piece.
She died. He lived (the man in the fields),
the child got by on a crust
and lived to be thirty, with sons. In the end
we came to be born too. Just.

Getting the Strap

The Our Father, the moment of fear.
He dodged round us and ran,
but was fetched back again
to stand before us on the platform.

The Our Father, the moment of fear
as the fist gripped and he hung
from the headmaster's arm,
doubling on the spot like a rabbit
blind for home.

The Our Father, the moment of fear.
The watch he'd stolen was given
back to its owner, dumb
in the front row, watching the strapping.

The Our Father, the moment of fear.
The strap was old and black and it cracked
on belly buttock and once across his lip
because he writhed and twisted.
He would not stand and take it.

The Our Father, the moment of fear.
There was a lot of sun
leaking through churchy windows
onto a spurt of urine.
After an age of watching
we sang the last hymn.

Gold

It was other girls who had gold.
Daddy's charm bracelet, added to
yearly, a corgi for Christmas.

They wore earstuds, not earrings.
They spent hours over small pains:
piercing and depilation.

They had watches for their eighteenths
because they might as well have their fun
to the sound of gold ticking.

It was hard to love them.
They liked sports cars, disasters,
other people's abortions,

and the men they married,
who buy them gold brooches
after longer than expected absences
and say, not *I love you*
but *I do love you* –

Adders

This path is silky with dust
where a lizard balances across bracken fronds
and a brown butterfly opens wide
to the stroke of the sun,

where a trawler feels its way along the sandbanks
and two yachts, helplessly paired, tack far out
like the butterflies which have separated and gone quiet.

A wild damson tree bulges with wasps
among heaps that are not worth picking,
and there a branch splits white with the lightning
of too heavy a harvest.

The lizard is gone in a blink.
Its two-pronged tail – half withered, half growing –
flicks out of the sun.
For a moment the pulse in its throat
keeps the grass moving.

A grass-bound offering of yarrow,
rosebay willow herb and veined convolvulus
lies to one side of the path
as if someone's coming back.
Instead, the sift of the dust –
beneath the bracken these hills are full of adders.

The West Coast

Here we are on the west coast.
There's so much earth under our feet –
silting – beach reclamation –
Dutch engineers pumping sand up
after the floods.
Sunday after Sunday we'd go there – our beach –
our kids in red crackling rainwear
the bite of wind at our ears.

Do you remember us on that coach to the rally –
was it Trafalgar Square or some other
crowd-flooded 'peaceful demonstration' –
the boom of mikes, and was it Frankie Armstrong
or someone else singing?
You were thirty, I was twenty-three.

In the hotel we went to for an hour and quarter
each Thursday, I was boring
putting *I Got You Babe* on the jukebox,
wishing I had some clothes,
talking about poems.
We swapped babysitting
with a friend who told me once when we got home
she'd tried to breastfeed my son
but he wouldn't stop crying.

We've left all that on the east coast,
like a drowned village with bells ringing.
Are we still getting married deep
under the sea, for the third time
and will it be lucky? People think
before they know us, this is our second marriage,
but we've married each other twice.

We were confident because we knew nothing,
If we'd known then how quickly the sun moves
could we have slowly set up everything
the way everyone does?
When we lived in the east
we had a game of looking at gravestones
on walks with the children –
mine had an angel's head
yours, I think, varied –

We plan your fiftieth birthday party now
for three years' time.
You're always breaching barriers
seven years before me, and the sea-wall's down,
but in the dark
you choose burial for me, can't bear
the thought of burning, tell me
you need to know where I am.

In our hearts everyone's gone –
the friends, the children.
What are these decisions we're making?
The east breaks up in us like polar ice.
Let's see, darling, let's see
who sleeps and who lies waking.

The conception

In the white sheets I gave you
everything I am capable of –
at the wrong time
of the month we opened
to the conception,

you were dewed like a plum
when at two am
you reached under the bed
for a drink of water adrift
in yesterday's clothes,

our sheets were a rope
caught between our thighs,
we might easily have died
but we kept on climbing.

Scan at 8 weeks

The white receiver
slides up my vagina,

I turn and you've come,
though I'm much too old for this
and you're much too young.

That's the baby
says the radiographer.
You are eight millimetres long
and pulsing,

bright in the centre of my much-used womb
which to my astonishment
still looks immaculate.

You are all heart,
I watch you tick and tick

and wonder
what you will come to,

will this be our only encounter
in the white gallery of ultrasound

or are you staying?
One day will we talk about this

moment when I first saw your spaceship
far off, heading for home?

Answering Machine

I leave my answering machine switched on.
I know there are messages coming in
but I'm plugged to my Walkman,
selecting the next tape
having just flicked off the radio.
A writer's surroundings must be carefully chosen.
News on the hour is the worst kind
of invasion of personal space.
I don't want my atmosphere broken.

There's a click then my voice,
with a veneer of friendliness
as it fends off the world
while pretending to give it a choice.
*'If you would like to leave a message
speak clearly after the long tone.'*
I'll whizz through later, fast-forwarding
and if I want, I'll get back to them.
After all, this is my home.

Later, the machines become silent.
My last page clatters from the printer
while I think about something to eat.
That new Italian bread from Waitrose,
Brie, coffee, a peach...
After such a good session
I deserve a little treat.
Yards of stuff spew from the fax
half-way down the hall – ridiculous.
Nothing can be as urgent as that.

My answering machine is packed,
ready for milking,
its red light exhaustedly winking.
I will play it back.
There is a huge whispering
like the voices of a thousand children
praying I am at home.
They are at the park, it is late,
there is a man watching them.
Too shy to talk to machines
they fade. What I have on my tape
is a dew of flesh, dissolving.

Pedalo

She swam to me smiling, her teeth
pointed by salt water, her mouth

a rock-pool's spat-out wine gum,
and then the tide flung

over her threshold,
and her lips moved.

The valve of her mouth was plumed
with salt-sweet tendrils,

sea danced from her pelt
of oil and muscle,

she rested her elbows on my pedalo
and there she hung

browning the pads of her shoulders
like a snake in the sun.

On shore thunderhead pines
drifted and swelled
like August umbrellas
stunning the fronts of hotels.

The sharp tide rinsed
over her threshold
as she dived once
and an angler cast
with lightning-proof rod
from the crinkled rocks.

A slow Medusa tilted beneath her,
shadowing toes and ankles
then on with its belly to the south,
braille on its tentacles.
She could read it like a newspaper
as it hunted alongside her.

I shivered
at the roll of her syllables,
and her joined feet winnowing,

and so I trawled her with me
over a shallow forest of dog-jawed
fruit sucking the trees,

past angler-fish socketing sand
with stone-cold faces,
through shrimps which divided bctween them
her armpit crevices

then flicked that way and this
tasting the dew of her breasts.

I trawled her past innocent sand
and the spumy outstretched arms
of agar and tangle –
but no, I wouldn't look down

however she called to me
until my fingers were shrunk
like old laundry.

I did not dare look down
to be snagged by ruby and seal-black
trees relaxing their weave.

On shore nobody's waiting.
The children, firm and delicious
as morning goods, have sheathed up their spades.

The boy with burned legs
has stepped out of his pantaloons
and skips in his blue vest
on the verandah boards.

The big one lights a mosquito candle,
Dad fills his glass of wine
four times, while they count,

and crickets saw in the ditch, frantic
along with the old car number-plate
and the boys' jar of fishing maggots.

They are screeching, all of them:
night, night, night's come
and no one's ever had a pedalo out this long.

Night-wind sifts on the shore
where striped recliners and wind-breaks
squeak by the green pavilion
crying for more.

I've lost my wife to the sea
Dad thinks hazily,
and takes another bottle of Muscadet
out of the gas cooler,

he imagines her dreaming
and sleeping miles from him,

each breath takes her farther,
toes in the air,

sea claps under her pedalo
impudently happy –

Below me now a mirror of wave-ruts
in firm brown sand,
I'd pulled her with me for miles
and there was nowhere to hide.

Now let me see you swim back
I said. She was mouthing
like mackerel tossed in a bucket
when the man's too busy to kill it,

with her scale-lapped bathing-hat
fly-blown and crazing.
She had nothing on underneath.
She was bare and bald as an eel.

Now she was an old bathing-woman
a mackintoshed marine Venus,
now she was that girl with lipstick
a push-up bra and a beehive,

now she was a slippery customer at Cannes
bare-breasted and young,
now she was my old
familiar snake again.

I took her curls in my hands and I pulled
but they were limpetted, smiling,
and there were just the two of us rocking.

We were close as spies
and she stayed silent
till day dived after its horizon
and the sea rustled with moonlight.

Swell shuts and opens
like a throat,

she claps
under my pedalo
impudently happy.

Where are you now
my sister, my spouse?

Clap with one hand
or clap to nothing –
I know you can.

Kiss me with the kisses of your mouth
my sister, my spouse.

The pedalo rocks
and is still again.

Calais

Calais, she says. That Queen
with her disappointed mouth
who is sallow in lime-green.
If you opened her breast after her death

you would find it written upon her heart
in secret. You know how she wants
you to tear her breastbone apart
and delve in through her lungs.

It will leave you with a catch in your breath
when you see the scar upon her heart
and the ribbony edge of her green silk dress
made brown by her blood.

Calais, she says, and it hurts
like the dead she buries and reburies,
like the pulse of life furred
in fat-packed arteries.

A spring tide bulges round Calais, the sea
spills and heaps into foam.
Open my heart, she breathes,
and you'll find it written,

this is what I hid, this is where I bled
this is what it cost me.
The tears swallowed, my blank face offered
to the incision of history.

It's there in the flesh, that chance
missed, and the scar of it.
For her it was a seaport in France,
I need not look so far for it.

Beetroot Soup

Its big red body ungulps
from the bowl in the fridge
with a fat shiver.

Glazed
with yellow beading of grease
the soup melts from the edge,

yesterday's beetroot
turns the texture of tongues
rolling their perfect ovals
out of the silt at the bottom.

Like duck breast-feathers, the dumplings
wisp to the surface, curl
as the soup brightens
just off the boil.

There'll be pearl onions
– two to a mouthful –
white butter,
then later

plums
piled in a bucket
under the table
thatched with dull leaves
and a black
webbing of twig
over their round
sleep.

When the soup's done
yellow
constellations
burst on its skin,

bread goes to work
wiping and sopping

the star-scum
set in a slick

on the base of the pot –
chicken fat.

The Diving Reflex

Where the great ship sank I am,
where cathedrals of ice breathe through me
down naves of cold
I tread and roll,

where the light goes
and the pressure weighs
in the rotten caves of an iceberg's side
I glide,

I am mute, not breathing,
my shoulders hunched to the stream
with the whales, drowsing.

Bells rang in my blood
as I went down
purling, heart over heel
through the nonchalant
fish-clad ocean –

her inquisitive kiss
slowed me to this
great cartwheel.

Down I go, tied to my rope.
I have my diving reflex to sister me,
and the blubbery sea cow
nods, knowing me.

There is blood in my veins
too thick for panic,
there is a down
so deep a whale
thins to a sheet of paper
and here I hang.
I will not drown.

*The diving reflex can enable the human body to shut down and maintain
life for as long as forty minutes underwater at low temperatures.*

Lilac

(for Gareth)

I had been worrying about your heart,
about a clog in its branches,

a knot in the age where we live
visiting people we love.

Alzheimers in the medical ward –
they shouldn't be here – but what can we do?

What can you do? You go outside
to the concrete patio shielded by dustbins

and fiercely read books. Like the doctors
(who haven't the cash for rehabilitation)

you should put money where your mouth is.
Chapter 7 says buy extra virgin

olive oil and not butter from now on.
You could go along with this.

They need to clear your heart with balloons
but they must wait for the funds,

meanwhile you walk down the street
carrying an armful of lilac

bunched, veined, tender,
so scented it makes you tremble.

Bathing at Balnacarry

Two miles or so beyond
the grey flank of the farm
and the wall of gravestones
the oncoming rain
put an edge on the mountains,

they were blue and sure
as the blade of a pocket knife
whizzed to a razor traverse
cutting the first
joint of my thumb –

It was stitched, not bleeding,
the dark threads in the sea were weeds
and my son was packing them
between the stones of his dam.

He was holding back the river
while the mountain punctured clouds
to hold back rain
no farther off than we'd cycled
bumping towards our swim.

In the grey purse of Balnacarry
there were red pebbles and smooth pebbles
and the close grain of the water,

the men were absent –
one walking in the woods
one fishing off the rocks –

the child behind me built up his dam
through which the downpour would blossom
in the sea at Balnacarry –
it was cold, but not lonely
as I stripped and swam.

From the Caravan

(for Catherine and Lydia)

Branches in the granite garden
pull back their sleeves of mist,

quiet as tired flesh
the sea moves against the cliffs,

in a heap in the caravan
kneeling up at the window
two children
time the foghorn.

Like seaweed flat on the sand
waiting for the tide
in wetsuits the surfers
wait in vans for the wind to rise.

The girls put dolls to sleep in envelopes.
There is the murmur of what the dolls do
from two separate picnic tables,

there is eating and drinking and going
out to be licked by mist.

Bare legs in the grass, montbretia
lighting the grey hedge
and shining off separate wet
spears of toadflax.
Everything is miniature
and sharp as insects.

The sea no longer exists
but the foghorn
curls its arms round the caravan
near as a cow's cough.

'We could see if you turned the mist off'
the dolls announce
as they play more frantically
tearing the paper.

The Lily Walk

At the start of the lily walk with my Japanese friend,
testing the wobble of the planks
as they knock out ripples, lightly
leashed with black twine,

a little water bubbles and pocks
to the blind nudging of giant carp
there are silver scales on the wood,
and the planks rock.

We are caught in an estuary of lilies.
Not only is it beautiful, it must be travelled.
Our only way is the lily path.

As we look new buds are rising,
their wet points tipped with mauve and cyclamen,
strongly rising through the water
like shut-eyed divers, hands in front of them,
into the tangle of lilies already blooming.

My friend in her black trousers
puts her weight on the wood, withdraws it,
but water seeps through the soles
of her cotton sandals.
Slowly, slowly, we go forward.

Now we are tightrope walkers above the sea of lilies
turned up to us like faces,
opening wide as if we were suns,
arching back their petals
to show us their pollen.

The noiseless clapping of lilies follows our footsteps.
We are far from land, lost to the hiss of reeds,
a bare finger-tip from one another.
I hear the scuff of my friend's trousers,
I watch her balancing hands call up more lilies.

Boys on the Top Board

Boys on the top board
too high to catch.
Noon is painting them out.

Where the willow swans
on the quarry edge
they tan and sweat

in the place of divers
with covered nipples –
Olympians,

that was the way of it.
Boys in the breeze
on the top board

where the willow burns
golden and green
on feet grappling –

boys fooling
shoulder to shoulder,
light shaking.

The lake's in shadow,
the day's cooling,
time to come down –

they stub their heels on the sun
then pike-dive
out of its palm.

Sylvette Scrubbing

Sylvette scrubbing,
arms of a woman
marbled with muscle
swabbing the sill,

tiny red grains
like suck kisses
on Sylvette's skin,
Sylvette's wrists
in and out of the water
as often as otters.

She grips that pig of a brush
squirts bristle
makes the soap crawl then
wipes it all up.

Babes in the Wood

Father,
I remember when you left us.
I knew all along
it was going to happen.
You gave me bread but wouldn't look at me
and Hansel couldn't believe it
because you were his hero,
but I loved you and knew
when you stroked my hair you were bound to leave us.

It was Hansel who crumbled the bread
while I skipped at your side and pretended
to prattle questions and guess nothing.

Father,
did you drive home quickly or slowly,
thinking of your second family
waiting to grab your legs with shrieks of *'Daddy!'*
and of your new wife's face, smoothing
now she sees you're alone?

Father,
we love it here in the forest.
Hansel's got over it. I've learned to fish
and shoot rabbits with home-made arrows.
We've even built ourselves a house
where the wolves can't get us.
But wolves don't frighten us much
even when they howl in the dark.
With wolves, you know where you are.

Cajun

This is what I want –

to be back again
with the night to come –

slipper-bags across our saddles
how fast we rode
and all for nothing.

Your lips on his lips
your hand in his hand
as you went from the dance.

We heard Mass at dawn,
When I knelt for communion

it was the hem of your white dress
I felt in my mouth,

it was your lips moving.

This is all I want

to be there again
with the night to come –

meet me where the fire
lights the bayou

watch my sweat shine
as I play for you.

It is for you I play
my voice leaping the flames,

if you don't come
I am nothing.

Bride on the Northern Line

Bride in the dark
shakes out her copper coins
sheds them one by one.
They are worth nothing
and here's the head of the bridegroom
pushing above its shirt collar,
sprung from bare earth
veined like a crocus –
she will not touch him.

Bride in the dark
with her dowry of change
paying her passage along the line,
but the train does not come.
The gutter is above her,
also the newsvendors
with their photos of disappearances.
A trail of sewers lined with condoms
runs to the eely rivers of London.

All he wanted was what was right –
to put rubber inside her.
Once she was earthed, he would have her.
Down the outmoded wooden escalator
they dance, unable to go faster,
catching their wedding-clothes
against a saxophonist's begging bowl.
She will come on him in the dark like a snowfall,
change him to nothing at all.

The Circle Line

It was a game children played.
There was no up or down line,
or being torn from cargoes of sleep
to the dawn of a destination.
There was only going round.

I could ride with you forever
said the hurdy gurdy of stations,
and a kiss could ripen from Aldgate
to the terraces of Bayswater
in the mouths of moneyless lovers.

For there was only going round:
the drunk in his hour of bliss,
the sleepers bombed-out by dreams,
the daring school children
all took their seats on the Circle Line.

Then I think how the train

Then I think how the train
from being a far blue point
troubling the slick of track
like thought in the dead of night
with a rack of stations between
the pulse of it and me

suddenly breathes at my back.
The platform stammers
and I see my poems
and see my youth in my poems
look up and back – then I think how the train

argues with a cloud of flowers
and always wins
cutting away with its cargo
leaving me in the carpark.

I tack the tarmac with footmarks
but now the train
switches its tail
shaking the rails,

then I think how the train
was waiting for me, a mushroom
put there for my hand
in the cow-coloured dawn.

That far blue point
how fast it's grown
having visited each one of the rack of stations
and found no one home.

How quick you are, I think to the train,
how near you've come.

Poem for Henry

A sharp bright starling with all
its wits about it, knowing
something had happened,

a bank of snow turning blue
in the cold evening
and the bus wheezing

and all the people who weren't yet
aunts, grandparents,
your baby father, drew

one step closer, patient as dots
which only seem not to move –
only waiting as the bus

ground the snow loose
only waiting to become
with everyday suddenness

what you'd make them.
What you haven't seen
can't matter:

the gas fire, the constellation
of girls' names fading,
your father sleeping

like you, now, then,
as the bus roars off and the boy's
a boy after three daughters,

shaken we guess
by that same snowstorm
which stops as it chooses –

soon it'll freeze. The girls
bob to the window. They close
the curtains and don't wake anyone.

In the Tube

I have a house and a handbag,
a pack of Quickies, an invitation.
I am all set up for a trip to London.

I would rather not walk down the stairs
which smell of urine, but then
the lift hurts my ears.

I read the advertisements
as I glide down escalators
men offer me tights and perfume –

I would like to be theirs.
I would like to watch films
about things they have done.

I would like to take part in a season
of dreams about Marlene Dietrich.
I would not like to be rich

because it would make me a target.
I might get fed to the pigs.
That young man opposite

with the Nike bag at his feet
is about to tell me he is a terrorist
then smile, and get off

just as the doors squeeze shut.
I always keep my eyes open.
I could tell he had an Irish accent

just by looking at him.
Now they have sealed the train
and we are behind time.

There is a face at the windows
which bulge out and in.
The air is falling.

I am in the Tube, I am holding
tight to my handbag, I'd like
to get out my Quickies.

Should I wait for the next station?
Should I call for attention?

Skips

If I wanted totems, in place of the poles
slung up by barbers, in place of the clutter
of knife-eyed kids playing with tops and whips,
and boys in cut-down men's trousers
swaggering into camera,
I'd have skips.

First, red and white bollards
to mark the road-space they need.
A young couple in stained workwear
– both clearly solicitors –
act tough with the driver, who's late.
The yellow god with its clangorous emptiness
sways on the chains.
The young man keeps shouting *BACK A LITTLE!*
as the skip rides above his BMW.
The driver, vengeful, drops it askew.

Next, the night is alive with neighbours
bearing their gifts, propitiations
and household gods – a single-tub washing-machine,
a cat-pissed rug, two televisions.
Soundless as puppets, they lower them
baffled in newspaper, then score
a dumbshow goal-dance to the corner.

The Caesarian Birth Experience
(lines written after a booking)

What a gig.

Lights, heat, nudity, even
splashes of blood on the sound system.
Here it comes again.

What a band.

Let's hear it for the Caesarian Birth Experience.
It's got style, it's got guile,
it doesn't even try to make sense.
As for the drugs – wild.
In the veins, in the spine
needles in more places
than you've ever imagined.

But if you don't want to catch that sound
of needles and knives
et cet
going for it
(you bet)
just put Jerry Lee Lewis on the headphones
and howl along.

Time by Accurist

Washed silk jacket by Mesa
in cream or taupe, to order,
split skirt in lime
from a selection at Cardoon,
£84.99,
lycra and silk body, model's own,
calf-skin belt by Bondage, £73.99,
tights from a range at Pins,
deck-shoes, white, black or strawberry,
all from Yoo Hoo,
baby's cotton trousers and braces
both at Workaday
£96.00; see list for stockists.

Photographs by André McNair,
styled by Lee LeMoin,
make-up by Suze Fernando at Face the Future,
hair by Joaquim for Plumes.
Models: Max and Claudie.
Location: St James Street Washeteria
(courtesy of Route Real America
and the Cape Regis Hotel),

baby, model's own,
lighting by Sol,
time by Accurist.

The Silent Man in Waterstones

I shall be the first to lead the Muses to my native land
VIRGIL

The silent man in Waterstones
LOVE on one set of knuckles
HATE on the other
JESUS between his eyes
drives his bristling blue skull
into the shelves,
thuds on CRIME / FANTASY
shivers a stand of Virago Classics
head-butts Dante.

The silent man in Waterstones
looks for a bargain.
Tattered in flapping parka
white eyes wheeling
he catches
light on his bloody earlobes
and on the bull-ring
he wears through his nose.

The silent man in Waterstones
raps for attention.
He has got Virgil by the ears:
primus ego in patriam mecum...
He'll lead the Muse to a rat-pissed underpass
teach her to beg
on a carpet of cardboard
and carrier bags.

The Wardrobe Mistress

This is the wardrobe mistress, touching
her wooden wardrobe. Here is her smokey
cross of chrysanthemums
skewed by the font.

They have put you in this quietness
left you here for the night.
Your coffin is like a locker
of mended ballet shoes.

You always looked in the toes.
There was blood in them, rusty
as leaves, blood from ballerinas.
Tonight it is All Souls

but you'll stop here quietly,
only the living have gone to the cemetery
candles in their hands
to be blown about under the Leylandii.

In your wooden wardrobe, you're used to waiting.
You know these sounds to the bone:
they are showing people to their seats
tying costumes at the back.

Everything they say is muffled,
the way it is backstage.
A stagehand pushes your castors
so you glide forward.

You know Manon is leaning
on points against a flat,
nervously flexing
her strong, injured feet,

you're in position too, arms crossed,
touching your bud of wood.
You needn't dance, it's enough
to do what you always did.

That was the second bell. You feel it
tang through the crush. The wind
pours on like music
drying everyone's lips,

they're coming, your dancers.
You hate the moment of hush.
There. The quick luck-words
knocking on wood.

When You've Got

When you've got the plan of your life
matched to the time it will take
but you just want to press SHIFT / BREAK
and print over and over
this is not what I was after
this is not what I was after,

when you've finally stripped out the house
with its iron-cold fireplace,
its mouldings, its mortgage,
its single-skin walls
but you want to write in the plaster
'This is not what I was after,'

when you've got the rainbow-clad baby
in his state-of-the-art pushchair
but he arches his back at you
and pulps his Activity Centre
and you just want to whisper
'This is not what I was after,'

when the vacuum seethes and whines in the lounge
and the waste-disposal unit blows,
when tenners settle in your account
like snow hitting a stove,
when you get a chat from your spouse
about marriage and personal growth,

when a wino comes to sleep in your porch
on your Citizen's Charter
and you know a hostel's opening soon
but your headache's closer
and you really just want to torch
the bundle of rags and newspaper

and you'll say to the newspaper
'This is not what we were after,
this is not what we were after.'

Afterword

Forty is an good age for thinking about the body. These poems were written in three and a half years or so between thirty-seven and forty, and if there is an underpinning web to this collection, if there is a conversation going on between the poems which is more than the sum of what each poem is saying, then I think it is to do with the body.

Sexuality, ageing, death, reproduction – these are all so much more relative than we think when we confront them first as absolutes in childhood or adolescence. At forty I find myself living in a time of almost overwhelming physical change. The first swathe has been cut through contemporaries by sickness, accident and death. Now ours is the generation that organises funerals: funerals of parents, funerals of colleagues and mentors who were thirty or more years older and have suffered that strange thing called a natural death. We have to watch weakness in those who were strong, and strength developing in the dependent. People in the rich West stay late-middle-aged for so long now. The years tick on and then suddenly, astonishingly, the world narrows to a white bed and the wink of the electrocardiograph. Our children are growing fiercely, claiming their own sexuality, taking up more room in the house than we dare to do. Their skin and hair and smiles bloom breathtakingly.

And those familiar bones in the mirror are covered by flesh which is beginning to change in ways I scarcely understand. No longer the youngest person on the bus, no longer automatically raked by male eyes in public places, no longer constantly made conscious of who I am and where I am by whistles and comments. *Go on darling, give us a smile.* Now I can forget how to smooth my face to unresponsive blankness in public or how to walk past building-sites with apparent unconcern. There's great freedom in this, and a powerful sense of recovering a body which for years seemed to belong as much to other people as to me.

The instability of the body is a source of comedy too. It swells and shrinks, presents itself one day as beautiful, the next as awkward and unsure. It sweats for fitness to stave off an autumn which is already wrinkling the edges of the leaves. It relishes an intimate, unshared life of snores, farts, bum-reducing exercises, masturbation and nose-picking, then walks out into public immaculately sheathed in whatever appearance suits it that day. The flesh-pinching reality of our bodies is constantly undermined by their surreality.

A late pregnancy has concentrated these thoughts in me. A woman of forty begins to look back on nearly thirty years of menstrual cycles, of the fear of pregnancy or the hope of pregnancy, of being always somewhere in a hormonal pattern which is both private and socially significant. Ahead of her is the menopause with its promise of a stability not experienced since childhood. And yet suddenly the body proves itself fertile again, capable of re-engaging in that flux of making bright, new creatures to walk out into the world clothed in flesh. Suddenly I am sitting at the word-processor with two hearts beating inside me.

There is a darker side to the past three years and to the poems. In public places bodies lie on damp concrete, wrapped in blankets and newspapers. Nothing is private – not the shivering nor the open-mouthed sleep nor the need which has to be exposed so that it can be ignored. Bare tattooed flesh on cold November days, shaven heads and pierced faces: these say what can be said with a body and without words except for the ritualised plea for spare change. This is the counterpoint to every trip to town, every humping of groceries into the car boot for the trip home. When I was little and there were no beggars on the streets I read of Victorian children shivering in doorways on Christmas Eve and wondered how anyone could bear to walk past, could refrain from opening their pockets and the doors of their warm houses. Now I know.

TV and radio hammer out a moment-by-moment account of wars we engage in or hold back from. Crackly voices tell of flesh melting in bunkers which the snout of a smart missile has penetrated. I am told of the battle about to start, the one which will transform living bodies to shreds of flesh and will use giant earth-movers to heap sand over them until they are obliterated. We are forced into a conspiracy where we inhabit the same time as sufferings which we pay our taxes to inflict, but cannot alleviate. As we spectate we combine physical immunity with a profound, grievous sense of complicity. In poems such as 'In the Desert Knowing Nothing' and 'Poem on the Obliteration of 100,000 Iraqi Soldiers', I have tried to express this without, I hope, seizing on the sufferings of others in order to demonstrate my own sensitivity.

Mandelstam wrote

> I have the present of a body – what should I do with it
> so unique it is and so much mine?

For me that question raises a hundred others. These poems are ways of finding forms for all these questions, rather than a set of answers.